A FIEL
OF
GREENS

African Gourmet
Slow Cooker Soups and Stews

Ivy Newton-Gamble

A Field of Greens front, back and interior pages designed by Ivy Newton-Gamble

www.TheAfricanGourmet.com

Printed in the United States

Special thanks to Pyramid Books

544-2 Gateway Blvd

Boynton Beach, Fl 33435

ISBN – 10: 1440407673

ISBN -13: 9781440407673

First edition

Welcome to
A Field of Greens

African Gourmet

Slow Cooker Soups and Stews

Preface

Years ago, I received a slow cooker as a present from my mother. Struggling though college, I was working part time while attending school fulltime. On a limited budget food, shopping usually meant I had to buy the inexpensive cuts of meats. At the urging of my mother one day I dusted off my slow cooker and created my very first meal, it was delicious! The meat was tender and juicy and the velvety buttery potatoes were heavenly. Ever since then the slow cooker and I have been best friends, creating memorable meals for family gatherings, potlucks and everyday meals.

Studying African history in college I learned that steaming and stewing of foods is a simple African cooking technique to soften tough foods. Naturally, my love of African history and cooking would meet at the crossroads and merge into one path leading me on the culinary journey of a lifetime. With over 80 simple recipes in the book A Field of Greens vegans, vegetarians, and meat lovers alike can enjoy a trip to Africa from the comforts of their own home. Besides wonderful recipes, I have also created this cookbook so that it will be as inviting just to sit down with and read just as well as creating fantastic meals for everyday cooking. The mouthwatering tempting collections of African recipes will delight family, friends, coworkers, and clientele. Broaden your mind and discover African cooking with A Field of Greens.

Dedication

To Thomas, Margaret, Lillian, Nika, Deja, Andrew, Carlton, Piedad, Heather, Solomon, and Bradford. Thank You.

African Regions and Countries

Eastern Africa

Burundi

Comoros

Djibouti

Eritrea

Ethiopia

Kenya

Madagascar

Malawi

Mauritius

Mozambique

Reunion

Rwanda

Seychelles

Somalia

Uganda

Tanzania

Zambia

Zimbabwe

Central (middle) Africa

Angola

Cameroon

Central African Republic

Chad

Congo

Democratic Republic of the Congo

Equatorial Guinea

Gabon

Sao Tome and Principe

Northern Africa

Algeria

Egypt

Libyan Arab Jamahiriya (Libya)

Morocco

Sudan

Tunisia

Southern Africa

Botswana

Lesotho

Namibia

South Africa

Swaziland

Western Africa

Benin

Burkina Faso

Cape Verde

Cote d'Ivoire

Gambia

Ghana

Guinea

Guinea-Bissau

Liberia

Mali

Mauritania

Niger

Nigeria

Saint Helena

Senegal

Sierra Leone

Togo

"However far a stream flows, it never forgets its origin"

–Yoruba Proverb

"The path is made by walking"

-African Proverb

"Many hands make light work"

-Tanzanian Proverb

Introduction

Quick and easy slow cooker meals are not usually associated with gourmet African cuisine. Whether you are a beginning chef or a seasoned professional, you can enjoy tasty easy soups and stews with simple recipes from all over the African continent. We all need recipes away from the mundane weeknight dishes. Fall in love with recipes that excite your entire family's culinary taste buds. From all over Africa this book helps you create recipes that are familiar, wholesome, tasty, and healthy. African soups and stews contain ingredients from fruits, vegetables, beef, lamb, chicken, shrimp, and fish from African coast to coast. The key attribute of African soups and stews is in the utilization of vegetables and starches since some African populations cannot afford meat. Meat is often a luxury associated with special occasions. Thickening soups and stews with cassava, legumes, sweet potatoes, yams etc. provides much needed substance. In some parts of Africa, meals are

served and eaten around large, communal bowls. Africa's geography is as diverse as its language, from the Sahara and

Kalahari deserts, tropical regions, subarctic snow-capped volcanic Mount Kilimanjaro, to savannas, plains, and rainforests. The range of climate and soil conditions in Africa has created a diversity of vegetables, fruits, wild and domesticated animals. Africa rests on both sides of the equator and is the only continent to extend from the northern temperate to southern temperate zones. The continent is surrounded by the Mediterranean Sea to the north, the Suez Canal and the Red Sea to the northeast, the Indian Ocean to the southeast, and the Atlantic Ocean to the west.

South African food has influences from indigenous Black tribes, Indians, Malaya, and Europeans. In East Africa, many hundreds of years ago, the Arabs settled on the coast, and Arabic influences are especially reflected with the use of sweet spices such as cinnamon, cloves and nutmeg. The British and Indians brought with them to Africa their curries and the technique of pickling to East Africa.

Asians introduced citrus fruits such as oranges, lemons, and limes. Portuguese introduced items like chilies, pineapples, and bananas. In North Africa, the Ottoman Turks brought sweet pastries and other bakery products. Central Africa's influence comes from the introduction of cassavas, peanuts, and pepper plants that arrived along with the slave trade. In West Africa the Portuguese, French, and British influenced regional cuisines with the introduction of plantains, citrus and pineapples, which are legacy of slave ship traffic between Africa and North America.

Religion also has a profound influence on food in Africa just as it does in the United States. Central Africa, is influenced by the Animist who have the belief that nature has a soul or  consciousness such as the mountains, trees, water etc..., Muslims believe pork consumption is taboo and avoid alcoholic beverages, Christian religions including Catholics and Protestants believe fasting and self denial develop religious restraint.

For people who enjoy cooking there is something satisfying about cooking a new healthy wholesome recipe for our loved ones to enjoy. The wonderful thing about African soups and stews is that you do not need a special occasion to create a wonderful hearty meal. Slow cookers allow the freedom to add a few ingredients and in little or no time, a warm, amazing scrumptious meal is ready to serve. All the recipes in this book have been adapted for the slow cooker and the directions are short and simple the recipes convenient and delicious. Some of the meats such as goat and ostrich may not be readily available at your local grocery store but ask your butcher and they may be able to special order your product.

In addition, online shopping is another resource to find exotic items such as pigeon and mutton. Finally, do not over look your local African, Caribbean and Latin grocery stores. These local stores have a wealth of new food products. Local farmers markets and grocery stores offer organic fruits and vegetables. If you are unable to grow fruits and vegetables yourself, look into organic produce for your family.

A Field of Greens offers well-known simple family friendly recipes that are delicious, healthy, and dependable. Most recipes are heart healthy and diabetic friendly. Quite a few recipes are also inexpensive allowing you to stretch your family food dollar. In two months time never repeat the same meal twice and create exciting extraordinary simple African gourmet meals with your slow cooker.

Slow Cooker Tips

1. All recipes in this book are designed for a 3 ½ -4 quart slow cooker and always follow the manufactures directions.

2. When using the recipes in this book add ingredients in the order they appear in the recipes.

3. Never use frozen foods in the slow cooker.

4. Every time you lift the lid, you lose heat especially if you are cooking on low therefore each time you lift the lid, extended cooking time 25- 30 minutes.

5. Fresh starchy root vegetables, such as yams, cassava pumpkin, plantains, onions, and sweet potatoes are usually placed in the bottom of the slow cooker, under the meat. The same holds true for vegetables such as turnips, collard greens, spinach and all forms of dry beans.

6. Remove skin from poultry and trim excess fat from meats before cooking to avoid extra fat.

7. Seafood should be cooked on high to avoid over cooking.

8. Add tender items such as tomatoes add the last hour if cooking on low or the last 30 minutes if cooking on high. Use precut vegetables to make prep easier.

9. Liquids do not readily evaporate in the slow cooker, remember vegetables are mostly liquid and will add to the moisture level in the recipes.

10. Each of the following recipes assumes all the ingredients are cleaned and prepped but remember before slow cooking, always rinse beans and remove any debris, wash all vegetables and rinse meat. Reduce cooking time by approximately one hour if cooking on high and 2 hours if cooking on low if using canned ingredients.

Sail into a new recipe voyage

Contents

African Spice Blends

Baharat (Ja! p.8)

Dukkah

Gabon Berbere

Fish Curry (Ja! p.10)

Harissa (Ja! p.12)

Malawi Curry

(Moroccan Spice (Ja! p.7))

Mit'mit'a

Ras El Hanout (Ja! p.9)

Eritrea Zrug

SWAHILI (SWAH-HEE-LEE) 101

Swahili is one of the official languages of Kenya, Tanzania, and Uganda.

Some common Swahili words are:

1. Via- Vine

2. Tafi- Fish

3. Stara- Modesty

4. Teto- Plea

5. Mto- River

6. Pima- Measure

7. Pondo- Pole

8. Ari -Pride

9. Banja- Break

10. Mafumbo- Enigma

(cf. Ja! p. 8)

Baharat

Algeria
Yield about 1/2 cup

Ingredients:

½ teaspoon lemon zest

1 tablespoon black peppercorns

1 tablespoon cinnamon

1 tablespoon ground coriander

1 teaspoon ginger

1 teaspoon paprika

½ teaspoon cloves

½ teaspoon nutmeg

2 tablespoons dried ground piri piri peppers

Directions:

1. mix all ingredients in a bowl
2. store in airtight container away from light and heat

Did you know: *Algeria is the second-largest country in Africa*

Dukkah

Egypt

Yield about 1/4 cup

Ingredients:

2 teaspoons sesame seeds

2 tablespoons finely chopped walnuts

1 teaspoon ground coriander

1 teaspoon cumin

1 teaspoon salt

1teaspoon white peppercorns

1 teaspoon crushed dried mint

Directions:

1. on medium heat in a small sauté pan dry roast seeds, nuts and peppercorns until slightly toasted
2. add all ingredients into a small bowl
3. store in airtight container away from light and heat

Did you know: *The capital of Egypt is Cairo*

Gabon Berbere

Gabon

Yield about 3/4 cup

Ingredients:

1 teaspoons ground cinnamon

1 teaspoon fenugreek seeds

1 teaspoon ground ginger

1 teaspoon ground nutmeg

1 teaspoon ground turmeric

1 teaspoon salt

½ teaspoon ground cloves

½ cup cayenne pepper

2 teaspoons ground cumin

1 tablespoon paprika

Directions:

1. mix all ingredients in a bowl
2. store in airtight container away from light and heat

Did you know: *Gabon is one of the more well to do stable African countries*

(cf. Ja! p.10)

Fish Curry
Ghana

Yield about 1/4 cup

Ingredients:

1 teaspoon sweet paprika

1 teaspoon coriander

2 teaspoons cumin

½ teaspoon nutmeg

2 teaspoons turmeric

2 teaspoons mustard seeds

Directions:

1. mix all ingredients in a bowl
2. store in airtight container away from light and heat

Did you know: *Ghana in 1957 became the first sub-Saharan country in colonial Africa to gain its independence*

(cf. Jal. p. 12)

Harissa
North Africa

Yield about ½ cup

Ingredients:

¼ cup dried ground piri piri peppers

2 cloves garlic, minced

1 teaspoon salt

1 teaspoon ground caraway

1 ½ teaspoon ground cumin

¼ teaspoon clove

1 teaspoon ground coriander

1 teaspoon crushed dried mint

3/4 cup olive oil

Directions:

1. place all ingredients into a food processor
2. grind to a paste and store in the refrigerator in an airtight container up to 3 weeks

Did you know: *Tunisia is somewhat larger than the state of Georgia*

Malawi Curry
The Republic of Malawi

Yield about 1/2 cup

Ingredients:

2 tablespoons cayenne pepper

1 teaspoon coriander

1 teaspoon ginger

1 teaspoon cardamom

½ teaspoon cloves

1 teaspoon cinnamon

2 teaspoons cumin

2 teaspoons turmeric

1 teaspoon fenugreek seeds

Directions:

1. mix all ingredients in a bowl
2. store in airtight container away from light and heat

Did you know: *The capital of Malawi is Lilongwe*

Mit'mit'a

Ethiopia

Yield about 1/4 cup

Ingredients:

2 tablespoons dried ground piri piri pepper

1 teaspoon cardamom

½ teaspoon cloves

1 teaspoon salt

Directions:

1. mix all ingredients in a bowl
2. store in airtight container away from light and heat

Did you know: *The capital of Ethiopia is Addis Ababa*

(cf. Jal p. 7)

Moroccan Spice

Morocco

Yield about 1/4 cup

Ingredients:

2 teaspoons black pepper

1 teaspoon dried garlic

1 teaspoon salt

1 teaspoon ground cinnamon

1 teaspoon ground coriander

1 teaspoon dried thyme

1 teaspoon ground ginger

1 teaspoon grated dried orange zest

Directions:

1. mix all ingredients in a bowl
2. store in airtight container away from light and heat

Did you know: *In Morocco, French often is the language of business, government, and diplomacy*

Ras El Hanout (finest spice blend)

Morocco

Yield about ½ cup

Ingredients:

2 teaspoons black pepper

1 tablespoon ground cardamom

1 teaspoon ground mace

1 teaspoon ground ginger

2 tablespoon dried ground piri piri pepper

1 teaspoon fennel seeds

1 teaspoon ground nutmeg

1 teaspoon ground allspice

1 teaspoon ground cinnamon

1 teaspoon ground cloves

1 teaspoon ground turmeric

Directions:

1. mix all ingredients in a bowl
2. store in airtight container away from light and heat

Did you know: *Morocco's lowest geographical point is Sebkha Tah about 180 feet below sea level*

Eritrea Zhug

Eritrea

Yield about ½ cup

Ingredients:

2 teaspoons dried ground piri piri

1 teaspoon ground coriander

2 teaspoons dried garlic

1 teaspoon mace

Directions:

1. mix all ingredients in a bowl
2. store in airtight container away from light and heat

Did you know: *Nakfa is the currency of Eritrea*

Basic Stocks

Vegetable Stock

Chicken Stock

Duck Stock

Fish Stock

Beef Stock

Lamb Stock

Goat Stock

MALAGASY (MAL-UH-GAS-EE) 101

Malagasy is a Malayo-Polynesian language and the national language of Madagascar.

Some common Malagasy words are:

1. Afo- Fire

2. Coco- Coconut

3. Dio- Clean

4. Foana- Always

5. Kolo- Care

6. Faly- Happy

7. Miaraka- Together

8. Vakoka- Cultural Heritage

9. Hahandro- Cook

10. Bombò- Sweet

Vegetable Stock

Yield 8 cups

Ingredients:

8 cups of water

5 cloves garlic crushed

2 large onions quartered

3 stalks celery cut in half

2 large carrots cut in half

1 cup fresh parsley

½ teaspoon black pepper

2 bay leaves

Directions:

1. combine all ingredients in a slow cooker
2. cover and simmer on high 3 ½ -4 hours or on low 7-8 hours or until carrots are tender when pricked with a fork
3. strain stock into a heatproof container discarding the solids

Did you know: *Ethiopia central mountain range is divided by Great Rift Valley, which is one of the world best coffee producing regions*

Chicken Stock

Yield 8 cups

Ingredients:

2 pounds chicken necks and backs

8 cups of water

3 cloves garlic crushed

1 large onion quartered

2 stalks celery cut in half

1 large carrots cut in half

½ teaspoon black pepper

2 bay leaves

Directions:

1. combine all ingredients in a slow cooker
2. cover and simmer on high 3 ½ -4 hours or on low 7-8 hours or until carrots are tender when pricked with a fork
3. strain stock into a heatproof container discarding the solids
4. after the stock cools place in refrigerator overnight then remove solidified fat from surface of stock and discard

Did you know: *Ghana has a tropical climate*

Duck Stock

Yield about 8 cups

Ingredients:

3 pounds duck necks, backs, and bones

8 cups of water

2 large onions quartered

½ teaspoon black pepper

Directions:

1. combine all ingredients in a slow cooker
2. cover and simmer on high 3 ½ -4 hours or on low 7-8 hours
3. strain stock into a heatproof container discarding the solids
4. after the stock cools place in refrigerator overnight then remove solidified fat from surface of stock and discard

Did you know: *Benin is slightly smaller than the state of Pennsylvania*

Fish Stock

Yield about 8 cups

Ingredients:

3 pounds fish heads, bones, tails

8 cups of water

3 cloves garlic crushed

1 large onion quartered

½ teaspoon black pepper

2 bay leaves

Directions:

1. combine all ingredients in a slow cooker
2. cover and simmer on high 3 ½ -4 hours or on low 7-8 hours
3. strain stock into a heatproof container discarding the solids

Did you know: *Africa is the second largest continent after Asia*

Beef Stock

Yield about 8 cups

Ingredients:

2 pounds beef soup bones

8 cups of water

3 cloves garlic crushed

1 large onion quartered

2 stalks celery cut in half

1 large carrots cut in half

½ teaspoon black pepper

2 bay leaves

Directions:

1. combine all ingredients in a slow cooker
2. cover and simmer on high 3 ½ -4 hours or on low 7-8 hours or until carrots are tender when pricked with a fork
3. strain stock into a heatproof container discarding the solids
4. after the stock cools place in refrigerator overnight then remove solidified fat from surface of stock and discard

Did you know: *The Sahara desert is the second largest desert after Antarctica*

Lamb Stock

Yield about 8 cups

Ingredients:

2 pounds lamb bones

8 cups of water

3 cloves garlic crushed

1 large onion quartered

2 stalks celery cut in half

1 large carrots cut in half

1 cup fresh parsley

½ teaspoon black pepper

2 bay leaves

Directions:

1. combine all ingredients in a slow cooker
2. cover and simmer on high 3 ½ -4 hours or on low 7-8 hours or until carrots are tender when pricked with a fork
3. strain stock into a heatproof container discarding the solids
4. after the stock cools place in refrigerator overnight then remove solidified fat from surface of stock and discard

Did you know: *Niamey is the capital of Niger*

Goat Stock

Yield about 8 cups

Ingredients:

2 pounds goat bones

8 cups of water

3 cloves garlic crushed

1 large onion quartered

2 stalks celery cut in half

1 large carrots cut in half

1 cup parsley

½ teaspoon black pepper

2 bay leaves

Directions:

1. combine all ingredients in a slow cooker
2. cover and simmer on high 3 ½ -4 hours or on low 7-8 hours or until carrots are tender when pricked with a fork
3. strain stock into a heatproof container throwing away the solids
4. after the stock cools place in refrigerator overnight then remove solidified fat from surface of stock and discard

Did you know: *The rupee is the currency of Seychelles*

Vegan and Vegetarian Soups

Pumpkin and Yam Soup

Botswana Cabbage

Peanut Butter Pumpkin Soup

Sweet Potato Soup

Cowpeas

Spinach Stew

Sukuma Greens

Plantains in Coconut Milk

Spicy Yam and Tomato Soup

Beet and Apricot Soup

Green Plantains

Nigerian Vegetable Soup

Orange Beet Soup

Groundnut Soup

Okra Stew

Spicy Avocado Soup

Shurit Ads

XHOSA (KOH-SUH) 101

Xhosa is one of the official languages of South Africa.

Some common Xhosa words are:

1. Ipapa- Porridge

2. Ne- Four

3. Ulale- Did you sleep

4. Bamba- Catch

5. Nase- The

6. Nzima- Hard

7. Fuya- Waste

8. Goba- Bend

9. Nini-When

10. Wela- Cross

ssava and Pinto Beans

of Africa

-5 servings

Ingredients:

1 cup dry pinto beans

2 cups cassava (Yucca) cut into even ½ " cubes

4 celery sticks, chopped

1 medium onion, sliced

2 ½ cups vegetable stock

Salt to taste

2 ripe tomatoes, sliced

Directions:

1. peel cassava and cut into even 1 inch chucks
2. add beans, cassava, celery, and onion into slow cooker
3. simmer on high 3-4 hours or low 6-8 hours or until the beans and cassava are soft
4. add tomatoes the last hour if cooking on low or 30 minutes if cooking on high

Did you know: *Gabon is a little smaller than the state of Colorado*

Fennel and Carrot Soup
North Africa

Yield 5-6 servings

Ingredients:

2 cloves of garlic crushed

3 cups baby carrots

2 tablespoons olive oil

1 chopped fennel bulb

1 cup vegetable stock

2 teaspoons fresh grated ginger

3 dried mint leaves

Salt to taste

Directions:

1. combine all ingredients in slow cooker
2. cover and simmer on low for 3-4 hours or high 1 ½ -2 hours or until carrots are tender when pricked with a fork
3. mash into a soup with a potato masher for a chunky texture or use a blender for a smooth texture

Did you know: *In Libya Arabic, Italian, and English, are all understood in the large city areas*

Pumpkin and Yam Soup

East Africa

Yield 6-8 servings

Ingredients:

1 ½ cups pumpkin cut into even ½ " cubes (substitute canned pumpkin)

1 ½ cups yam cut into even ½ " cubes (substitute canned yams)

1 clove garlic crushed

1 stick cinnamon

1 teaspoon salt

1 small piece fresh ginger root

2 cups vegetable stock

Directions:

1. cut pumpkin into 4 equal parts then peel with a vegetable peeler; remove fibrous membrane and seeds then cut into 1-inch cubes place in slow cooker
2. peel yams and cut into 1 inch cubes add to the slow cooker
3. then add garlic, cinnamon, salt, ginger and vegetable stock
4. cover and simmer on high for 3-4 hours or low for 6-8 hours, until vegetables are tender
5. remove ginger root, mash cooked ingredients with a potato masher for a chunky texture or a blender for a smooth texture

Did you know: *The capital of Somali is Mogadishu*

Botswana Cabbage

Botswana

Yield 6-8 servings

Ingredients:

2 cups sweet potatoes cut into even ½ " cubes

1 medium shredded green cabbage

1 tablespoon date and raisin chutney

1 cup baby carrots

½ of a sliced yellow onion

 Salt to taste

2 ½ cups vegetable stock

Topping:

1 cup shredded carrots

Directions:

1. peel sweet potatoes and cut into 1 inch cubes add to the slow cooker with shredded cabbage
2. cut unpeeled carrots into 1 inch circles , slice onion and add to the slow cooker with salt and vegetable stock
3. cover and simmer on high for 2-3 hours or low for 4-6 hours, until vegetables are tender
4. serve warm and top with shredded carrots if desired

Did you know: *English is the official language of Botswana*

Peanut Butter Pumpkin Soup

West Africa

Yield 4-6 servings

Ingredients:

1 small pumpkin peeled and seeded, cut into even ½ " cubes about 3 cups (Substitute canned pumpkin)

3 tablespoons creamy peanut butter

1 cinnamon stick

1 dried whole clove

1 dried whole allspice

¼ cup orange flower honey

2 cup vegetable stock

Salt to taste

Directions:

1. mix peanut butter, honey and stock well
2. cut pumpkin into 1 inch even cubes and add to slow cooker along with the remaining ingredients
3. mix ingredients well simmer on high for 2-3 hours or low for 4-6 hours
4. remove cinnamon stick and clove mash cooked ingredients with a potato masher for a chunky texture or use a blender for a smooth texture
5. top with ground peanuts if desired

Did you know: *One of the national holidays in Burkina Faso is Republic Day which is celebrated on December 11th*

Sweet Potato Soup

Central Africa

Yield 4-8 servings

Ingredients:

3 cups fresh peeled 1 " cubed sweet potatoes

½ cup raisins

½ cups dried plums

1 stick cinnamon

1 teaspoon salt

2 teaspoons peanut butter

2 cups vegetable stock

Topping:

1 cup shredded fresh sweet potato (optional)

Directions:

1. mix peanut butter and stock well
2. add cubed sweet potatoes, raisins, plums, cinnamon, peanut butter, salt and stock into a slow cooker simmer on high 2-3 hours or low 4-6 hour
3. mash into a soup with a potato masher for a chunky texture or use a blender for a smooth texture
4. garnish with the shredded sweet potatoes and serve warm

Did you know: *The capital of Chad is N'Djamena*

Cowpeas

All of Africa

Yield 4-6 servings

Ingredients:

1 cup dry black eyed peas

2 teaspoons piri piri pepper (substitute cayenne pepper)

1 sliced medium yellow onion

3 cups vegetable stock

1 small piece fresh ginger root

2 medium fresh tomatoes diced

1 cup chopped green onions

Salt to taste when cooking completes

Directions:

1. pour beans into slow cooker add pepper, sliced onion, vegetable stock, ginger and salt
2. cover and simmer on high for 3-4 hours or low for 6-8 hours, until beans are tender
3. add tomatoes the last hour if cooking on low or 30 minutes if cooking on high
4. remove ginger root and serve warm topped with chopped green onions
5. to thicken soup mash some of the cooked beans

Did you know: *The capital of Uganda is Kampala*

Spinach Stew

Morocco

Yield 3-5 servings

Ingredients:

2 cored gala apples cut into even ½ " cubes

2 cored granny smith apples cut into even ½ " cubes

3 cups fresh spinach

1 cup pine nuts

1 teaspoon coriander

1 teaspoon fresh grated ginger

1 cinnamon stick

½ cup vegetable stock

Salt to taste

Directions:

1. combine all ingredients in a slow cooker
2. cover and simmer on high for 2-3 hours or low for 4-6 hours or until apples are tender when pricked with a fork
3. remove cinnamon stick before serving

Did you know: *Morocco is slightly larger than the state of California*

Sukuma Greens

Tanzania

Yield 3-4 servings

Ingredients:

8 cups collard greens

1 large green bell pepper, chopped and seeded

½ cup onion, chopped

¼ cup lemon juice

1 clove of garlic crushed

2 cups vegetable stock

½ teaspoon salt

1 teaspoon curry powder

2 medium fresh tomatoes evenly sliced

Directions:

1. in a slow cooker add all the ingredients
2. cover and simmer on high for 4-5 hours or low for 8-10 hours, until greens are tender

Did you know: *The highest geographical point in Tanzania is Mount Kilimanjaro 19,340 feet*

Plantains in Coconut Milk

Kingdom of Swaziland

Yield 3-4 servings

Ingredients:

3 yellow plantains

1 teaspoon curry powder

1 cinnamon stick

½ teaspoon salt

2 cups coconut milk

1 cup vegetable stock

Directions:

1. peel plantains and cut into 1 inch circles
2. add remaining ingredients and simmer in a slow cooker on high 2 ½ -3 hours or low 5 -6 hours until plantains are fork tender
3. remove cinnamon stick and mash into a soup with a potato masher for a chunky texture or use a blender for a smooth texture

Did you know: *Swaziland is a touch smaller than the state of New Jersey*

Spicy Yam and Tomato Soup

Central Africa

Yield 4-5 servings

Ingredients:

3 cups unpeeled 1 " cubed yams

1 large green bell pepper, chopped and seeded

3 cloves garlic crushed

2 teaspoons olive oil

1 hot dried chili pepper

1 cup tomato juice

2 cups water

1 teaspoon turmeric

1 teaspoon allspice

½ teaspoon salt

¼ cup chopped fresh parsley

Directions:

1. in a slow cooker, add all the ingredients
2. cover and simmer on high for 2-3 hours or low for 4-6 hours, until yams are fork tender
3. mash into a soup with a potato masher for a chunky texture or use a blender for a smooth texture

Did you know: *Emi Koussi, a dormant volcano in the Tibesti Mountains, is the highest point in Chad*

Beet and Apricot Soup

South Africa

Yield 4-6 servings

Ingredients:

1 medium chopped onion

1 cup fresh peeled apricots (or dried apricots)

3 cups canned beets, drained

1 ½ cup vegetable stock

1 teaspoon grated ginger root

½ teaspoon salt

Directions:

1. place all ingredients into slow cooker
2. simmer on high for 1 ½ -2 hours or low for 3-4 hours, until apricots are tender
3. mash into a soup with a potato masher for a chunky texture or use a blender for a smooth texture

Did you know: *South Africa is the southernmost tip of the continent of Africa*

Green Plantains

Ghana

Yield 3-6 servings

Ingredients:

3 large green plantains peeled

2 tablespoons chopped garlic

2 tablespoons red pepper flake

1 tablespoon ground ginger

¼ cup diced onion

2 cups vegetable stock

1 lime cut into wedges (optional)

Directions:

1. slice the plantains down the center lengthwise ¾ the way though the plantation without cutting in half
2. in a food processor, pulverize peppers, garlic, ginger, oil and onions until a paste forms
3. gently open the slits on the plantains and pack with seasoning paste
4. pour vegetable stock on the sides of the plantains
5. simmer in slow cooker on high 2 ½ -3 hours or low 5 -6 hours until plantains are fork tender
6. top with lime wedges if desired

Did you know: *Ghana is slightly smaller than the state of Oregon*

Nigerian Vegetable Soup

Nigeria

Yield 6-8 servings

Ingredients:

3 cups spinach

8 cups turnip greens

¼ cup vinegar

3 cloves of garlic crushed

2 hot dried chili peppers

3 cups vegetable stock

½ teaspoon salt

2 medium fresh tomatoes evenly sliced

Directions:

1. in a slow cooker add all the ingredients except tomatoes
2. cover and simmer on high for 4-5 hours or low for 8-10 hours, until turnip greens are tender
3. add tomatoes the last hour if cooking on low or 30 minutes if cooking on high

Did you know: *English is the official language of Nigeria*

Orange Beet Soup

Morocco

Yield 4-6 servings

Ingredients:

4 cups drained canned beets

2 slices of an unpeeled blood orange

1 teaspoon Moroccan Spice Mix

½ cup orange juice

2 cups vegetable stock

Directions:

1. place all ingredients into a slow cooker
2. simmer on high for 1 ½ -2 hours or low for 3-4 hours
3. mash into a soup with a masher for a chunky texture or use a blender for a smooth texture

Did you know: *Morocco has a Mediterranean climate*

Groundnut Soup

Ghana

Yield 3-6 servings

Ingredients:

1 ½ cups raw shelled peanut, skins removed

3 cloves garlic crushed

1 medium chopped onion

1 teaspoon grated ginger root

2 ½ cups vegetable stock

1 teaspoon salt

1 dried hot chili pepper

Directions:

1. in a slow cooker, add all the ingredients
2. simmer on high for 2-3 hours or low for 4-6 hours

Did you know: *Ghana's Lake Volta is the world's largest artificial lake*

Okra Stew

West Africa

Yield 6-8 servings

Ingredients:

4 cups fresh okra

3 cloves garlic crushed

1 tablespoons lemon juice

2 cups vegetable stock

1 tablespoon caraway seeds

2 medium fresh tomatoes evenly sliced

Salt and pepper to taste

Directions:

1. in a slow cooker, add all the ingredients
2. simmer on high for 2-3 hours or low for 4-6 hours, until okra is tender
3. add tomatoes the last hour if cooking on low or 30 minutes if cooking on high

Did you know: *Burkina Faso is a little larger than the state of Colorado*

Spicy Avocado Soup

North Africa

Yield 4-5 servings

Ingredients:

3 large peeled, pitted avocados evenly sliced

2 cups vegetable stock

1 dried African bird pepper

2 teaspoons Baharat spice mix

½ teaspoon salt

1 tablespoon lemon juice

Topping:

Chèvre (goat cheese) optional

Directions:

1. peel and remove seed from avocados
2. add all ingredients except chèvre (goat cheese) to slow cooker simmer on high for 1-1 ½ hours or low for 2 ½ -3 hours
3. mash into a soup with a masher for a chunky texture or use a blender for a smooth texture
4. serve soup topped with a slice of chèvre (goat cheese) if desired

Did you know: *In Sudan desert dominates the northern landscape*

Shurit Ads

Egypt

Yield 4-5 servings

Ingredients:

1 cup red lentils

1 medium onion chopped

2 garlic cloves crushed

2 tablespoons olive oil

2 teaspoons Dukkah spice

2 cups vegetable stock

One 14 ounce can stew tomatoes

Directions:

1. add lentils, onion, cloves, olive oil, cumin, salt and stock
2. simmer in a slow cooker on high 3-4 hours or low 6-8 hours
3. add tomatoes the last hour if cooking on low or 30 minutes if cooking on high

Did you know: *Egypt is a little more than three times the size of New Mexico*

Chicken and Duck Stews

Tsebhi Derho

Doro Wat

Rosemary and Fig Tajine

Duck Breast with Quince

Kuku Paka

Date and Orange

Chicken Tajine

Curry Chicken and Apple Stew

Red Palm Oil Chicken Stew

Huku Ne Dovi

Duck And Ginger Stew

Senegalese Chicken Wings

Tanzania Chicken Stew

Mustard Chicken

Kumquat Chicken

Green Olives and Chicken Tajine

EBELE (UH-N-DUH-BEE-LEE) 101

ern Ndebele spoken in Zimbabwe and Southern Ndebele
uth Africa.

Some common Ndebele words are:

1. Fica- Find

2. Enza- Make

3. Dala- Create

4. Funa- Desire

5. Goba- Bend

6. Esula- Wipe off

7. Hamba- Move

8. Buza- Question

9. Zama- Try

10. Lula- Easy

Tsebhi Derho

Eritrea

Yield 4-8 servings

Ingredients:

2 split skinless chicken breasts

1 medium size onions, chopped

1 tablespoon butter

2 tablespoons lemon juice

2 teaspoons Eritrea Zhug

2 cups chicken stock

2 medium fresh tomatoes evenly sliced

3 peeled hard boiled eggs

Directions:

1. add all the ingredients except the tomatoes and eggs into the slow cooker
2. simmer on high 4-5 hours or low 8-10 hours
3. meanwhile hard-boil three eggs and set aside
4. add tomatoes the last hour if cooking on low or 30 minutes if cooking on high
5. peel and slice the hard-boiled eggs and serve as a garnish with the stew

Did you know: *The capital of Eritrea is Asmara*

Doro Wat

Ethiopia
Yield 4-8 servings

Ingredients:

4 skinless chicken thighs

1 cup chopped onion

2 teaspoons piri piri sauce (substitute cayenne pepper)

2 teaspoons ground paprika

2 teaspoons allspice

1 whole clove

1 tablespoon chopped thyme

2 cloves garlic chopped

1 teaspoon fresh ground ginger

2 cups chicken stock

One 14 ounce can stew tomatoes

Salt to taste

Directions:

1. in a slow cooker, add all the ingredients
2. simmer on high for 4-5 hours or low for 8-10 hours, until chicken is tender
3. add tomatoes the last hour if cooking on low or 30 minutes if cooking on high remove clove and serve

Did you know: *Ethiopia is the world's 27th largest country*

Rosemary and Fig Tajine

North Africa

Yield 4-8 servings

Ingredients:

2 skinless split chicken breasts

1 cup dried figs (three fresh whole figs)

1 small slice of orange

1 tablespoon dried rosemary

1 ½ cups chicken stock

Pepper to taste

Directions:

1. in a slow cooker, add all the ingredients
2. cover and simmer on high for 4-5 hours or low for 8-10 hours until chicken is tender

Did you know: *Libya is slightly larger than the state of Alaska*

Duck Breast with Quince

South Africa

Yield 2-4 servings

Ingredients:

2 split duck breasts

2 quinces evenly sliced

¼ cup wild flower honey

2 teaspoons fresh grated ginger

1 cinnamon stick

2 cups duck stock

Directions:

1. in a slow cooker add ingredients
2. simmer on high 3-4 hours or low 6-8 hours until duck is fork tender
3. remove cinnamon stick and serve

Did you know: *In 1948, the National Party was voted into power in South Africa*

Kuku Paka

East Africa

Yield 4-5 servings

Ingredients:

5 skinless chicken legs

1 onion chopped

1 green bell pepper seeded and chopped

3 cloves garlic crushed

1 teaspoon fresh ground ginger

1 tablespoon curry powder

1dried whole clove

2 teaspoons coriander

1 ½ cups chicken stock

One 14 ounce can stew tomatoes

1 cup coconut milk

Directions:

1. in a slow cooker, add all the ingredients, except the coconut milk
2. simmer on high for 4-5 hours or low for 8-10 hours, until chicken is tender
3. add the coconut milk the last hour if cooking on low or 30 minutes if cooking on high

Did you know: *Rwanda is the most densely populated country in Africa*

Date and Orange Chicken Tajine

Morocco

Yield 3-6 servings

Ingredients:

3 chicken legs

3 chicken thighs

1 onion chopped

½ cup pitted dates

1 cinnamon stick

1 teaspoon fresh ground ginger

1 teaspoon turmeric

1 tablespoon orange peel

1 ¼ cups chicken stock

¼ cup orange juice

Salt to taste

Directions:

1. in a slow cooker add all the ingredients
2. simmer on high for 4-5 hours or low for 8-10 hours, until chicken is tender
3. remove cinnamon stick and serve

Did you know: *Morocco's population is about 34,343,220*

Curry Apple Chicken Soup

Senegal

Yield 4-8 servings

Ingredients:

4 skinless chicken thighs

2 onions evenly sliced

1 cup diced celery

2 cored and sliced medium apples

1 cup raisins

1 cinnamon stick

1 tablespoon peanut butter

1 tablespoon curry powder

1 ½ cup chicken stock

Salt and pepper to taste

Directions:

1. mix peanut butter and stock well
2. in a slow cooker, add all the ingredients
3. simmer on high for 4-5 hours or low for 8-10 hours, until chicken is tender
4. remove cinnamon stick and serve

Did you know: *Senegal is slightly smaller than the state of South Dakota*

Red Palm Oil Chicken Stew

Angola

Yield 4-8 serving

Ingredients:

4 cloves garlic crushed

2 cups peeled yams cut into 1 " cubes

2 split skinless chicken breasts

2 teaspoons ground cumin

¼ cup Red Palm Oil

1 ½ cups chicken stock

Salt to taste

Directions:

1. in a slow cooker, add all the ingredients
2. simmer on high for 4-5 hours or low for 8-10 hours, until chicken is tender

Did you know: *The Kwanza is the currency of Angola*

Huku Ne Dovi

Zimbabwe

Yield 3-6 servings

Ingredients:

4 cups turnip greens chopped

3 skinless chicken thighs

3 cloves garlic crushed

2 onions evenly sliced

¼ cup creamy peanut butter

1 cup baby carrots

1 ½ cups chicken stock

Salt and black pepper to taste

Directions:

1. mix peanut butter and stock well
2. in a slow cooker, add all the ingredients
3. simmer on high 3-4 hours or low 6-8 hours until chicken and greens are tender

Did you know: *Zimbabwe is somewhat larger than the state of Montana*

Duck and Ginger Stew

Madagascar

Yield 4-8 servings

Ingredients:

4 cloves garlic crushed

2 split duck breasts

2 onions evenly sliced

2 teaspoons Baharat spice mix

1 ½ cups duck stock

Salt and black pepper to taste

Directions:

1. in a slow cooker, add all the ingredients
2. simmer on high 3-4 hours or low 6-8 hours until duck is fork tender

Did you know: *Madagascar is an island in the Indian Ocean and is mountainous in its center*

Senegalese Chicken Wings

Senegal

Yield 4-8 servings

Ingredients:

8 chicken wings, tips removed

3 cloves garlic crushed

2 tablespoons apple cider vinegar

½ teaspoon black pepper

2 teaspoons coriander

2 teaspoons paprika

2 teaspoons red pepper flake

2 teaspoons ground ginger

1 cup orange flower honey

2 cups chicken stock

Salt and pepper to taste

Directions:

1. in a slow cooker, add all the ingredients
2. simmer on high 3-4 hours or low 6-8 hours until chicken is fork tender

Did you know: *Senegal is the westernmost country on the African continent*

Tanzanian Chicken Stew

Tanzania

Yield 3-6 servings

Ingredients:

2 green plantains cut into 1 inch circles

3 cups chopped cabbage

3 skinless chicken thighs

1 cup chopped onions

1 tablespoon paprika

1 tablespoon cumin

2 cups chicken stock

Salt and pepper to taste

Directions:

1. in a slow cooker, add all the ingredients
2. simmer on high 3-4 hours or low 6-8 hours until chicken is fork tender

Did you know: *English is the official language of Tanzania and the primary language of higher education*

Mustard Chicken

Senegal

Yield 4-8 servings

Ingredients:

4 cloves garlic crushed

2 cups peeled yam cut into 1 " cubes

2 split skinless chicken breasts

1 cup chopped onions

1 tablespoon mustard seeds

2 tablespoons lemon juice

2 teaspoons piri piri sauce (substitute cayenne pepper)

1 ½ cups chicken stock

One 14 ounce can stew tomatoes

Salt and pepper to taste

Directions:

1. in a slow cooker, add all the ingredients
2. simmer on high 3-4 hours or low 6-8 hours until chicken is fork tender
3. add tomatoes the last hour if cooking on low or 30 minutes if cooking on high

Did you know: *Senegal is slightly smaller than the state of South Dakota*

Kumquat Chicken

North Africa

Yield 4-6 Servings

Ingredients:

2 large unpeeled sweet potatoes cut into 1 inch pieces

4 chicken legs

4 kumquats

1 cup chopped onion

2 teaspoons Berbere mix

2 cups chicken stock

Directions:

1. slice kumquats in half lengthwise and remove seeds, do not peel
2. in a slow cooker, add all the ingredients
3. simmer on high for 3-4 hours or low for 6-8 hours, until chicken is tender

Did you know: *In Tunisia the life expectancy is 75.56 years*

Green Olives and Chicken Tajine

North Africa

Yield 5-8 servings

Ingredients:

4 cloves garlic crushed

5 skinless chicken thighs

1 cup chopped onion

2 teaspoons chopped fresh ginger

2 teaspoons paprika

1 teaspoon ground turmeric

1 cinnamon stick

1 teaspoon lemon zest

2 cups chicken stock

1 cup canned pit green olives

Directions:

1. in a slow cooker, add all the ingredients except olives
2. simmer on high for 4-5 hours or low for 8-10 hours, until chicken is tender
3. add the olives the last hour if cooking on low or 30 minutes if cooking on high
4. remove cinnamon stick and serve

Did you know: *Sudan is slightly more than one-quarter the size of the US*

Seafood Stews

Apricot Citrus Fish

Curried Fish

Mtuzi Wa Samaki

Stewed Fish

Coconut Prawns

Pomegranate Trout

Cod with Fennel

King Fish Stew

Prawn and Kale Stew

ZULU (ZOO-LU) 101

Zulu is one of the official languages of South Africa and Swaziland.

Some common Zulu words are:

1. Enkulu- Large

2. Umuka- Line

3. Vala- Close

4. Woza- Come

5. Ifu- Cloud

6. Wena- You

7. Yebo- Yes

8. Yazi -Know

9. Leyo- That

10. Ifamu- Farm

Apricot Citrus Fish

South Africa

Yield 3-5 servings

Ingredients:

1 tablespoon olive oil

1 pound catfish fillets

1 cup chopped onion

1 cup dried apricots

2 teaspoons piri piri (substitute cayenne pepper)

1 cup fish stock

2 tablespoons grated lemon zest

Salt and pepper to taste

Directions:

1. in a slow cooker, add all the ingredients
2. simmer on high 1-1 ½ hours until fish is tender and flaky

Did you know: *South Africa has three capitals Pretoria is the administrative capital, Cape Town the legislative capital and Bloemfontein the judicial capital*

Curried Fish

Ghana

Yield 3-5 servings

Ingredients:

1 tablespoon olive oil

3 medium Tilapia filets

2 cloves minced garlic

1 cup chopped onions

2 teaspoons fish curry powder

1 cup fish stock

One 14 ounce can stew tomatoes

Directions:

1. in a slow cooker, add all the ingredients
2. simmer on high 1-1 ½ hours.
3. add tomatoes the last hour if cooking on low or 30 minutes if cooking on high

Did you know: *The nationality of Ghana is Ghanaian*

Mtuzi Wa Samaki

Kenya

Yield 2-3 servings

Ingredients:

1 tablespoon butter

2 cloves garlic crushed

3 thin slices of lime

1 cleaned medium yellow fin tuna (remove head and tail if desired)

1 large onion, sliced

2 tablespoons lime juice

1 teaspoon ground cumin

1 teaspoon ground coriander

1 teaspoon salt

1 cup fish stock

Directions:

1. stuff the fish with garlic and lime slices
2. add butter to the slow cooker then the fish
3. add all of the remaining ingredients
4. simmer on high 1-1 ½ hours until fish is tender and flaky

Did you know: *Kenya has two official languages English and Kiswahili*

Stewed Fish

Côte d'Ivoire

Yield 2-3 servings

Ingredients:

1 tablespoon olive oil

3 cloves garlic crushed

1 cleaned medium size red snapper (remove head and tail if desired)

2 cups okra cut into 1/4 " circles

½ cup parsley finely chopped

2 teaspoons cayenne pepper

1 med onion, chopped

2 teaspoons ground coriander

1 cup fish stock

One 14 ounce can stew tomatoes

Directions:

1. stuff fish with the garlic and parsley
2. add oil to the slow cooker then the fish
3. add all of the remaining ingredients simmer on high 1-1 ½ hours until fish is tender and flaky
4. add tomatoes the last hour if cooking on low or 30 minutes if cooking on high

Did you know: *Cote d' Ivoire celebrates Independence Day August 7th*

Coconut Prawns

Mozambique

Yield 4-6 servings

Ingredients:

5 cloves garlic crushed

1 tablespoon olive oil

1 pound cleaned prawns

½ cup parsley finely chopped

1 sprig thyme

2 teaspoons piri piri (substitute cayenne pepper)

2 teaspoons coriander

1 teaspoon mustard seeds

1 teaspoon black pepper corns

1 cup coconut milk

½ cup vegetable stock

Directions:

1. in a slow cooker, add all the ingredients
2. simmer on high 1-1 ½ hours or until prawns are pink

Did you know: *Mozambique Nationality is Mozambican*

Pomegranate Trout

South Africa

Yield 2-3 servings

Ingredients:

1 pomegranate

1 tablespoon olive oil

1 cleaned medium size trout (remove head and tail if desired)

4 slices of oranges

¼ cup unsalted almonds, chopped

½ cup chopped mint

2 teaspoons coriander

¼ cup pomegranate juice

1 cup fish stock

Directions:

1. cut open the pomegranate and remove the seeds
2. stuff the fish with half of the pomegranate flesh, oranges, almonds and mint
3. add oil to the slow cooker then the fish
4. add all of the remaining ingredients
5. simmer on high 1-1 ½ hours until fish is tender and flaky

Did you know: *South Africa is the world's largest producer of platinum, gold, and chromium*

Cod with Fennel

East Africa

Yield 4-6 servings

Ingredients:

1 tablespoon olive oil

1 pound cod filets

1 fennel bulb trimmed and chopped

2 teaspoons coriander

1½ cups fish stock

Salt and pepper to taste

Directions:

1. in a slow cooker, add all the ingredients
2. simmer on high 1-1 ½ hours or until fish is tender and flaky

Did you know: *French is one of the official languages of Djibouti*

Kingfish Stew

East Africa

Yield 2-4 servings

Ingredients:

1 tablespoon olive oil

3 cloves garlic crushed

2 medium kingfish steaks

1 cup chopped onion

2 teaspoons Ras El Hanout

1 cup fish stock

One 14 ounce can stew tomatoes

Salt and pepper to taste

Directions:

1. in a slow cooker, add all the ingredients
2. simmer on high 1-1 ½hours until fish is tender and flaky
3. add tomatoes the last hour if cooking on low or 30 minutes if cooking on high

Did you know: *Rwanda, like most African counties has several official languages, Kinyarwanda, French, and English*

Prawn Kale Stew

Cameroon

Yield 4-6 servings

Ingredients:

4 cups fresh kale

1 pound cleaned prawns

1 medium onion, chopped

1 tablespoon creamy peanut butter

2 cloves of garlic crushed

2 cups vegetable stock

2 teaspoons piri piri (substitute cayenne pepper)

½ teaspoon salt

Directions:

1. mix the stock and peanut butter well
2. in a slow cooker, add all the ingredients
3. simmer on high for 2 hours

Did you know: *Cameroon is a bit larger than the state of California*

Beef and Ostrich Stews

South African Bobotie

Seswaa

Kyinkyinga

Lamb and Chickpea Tajine

Rwandan Beef Stew

Beef Oxtail

Mushroom and Garlic Ostrich Stew

Beef and Cassava Stew

Beef and Vegetable Stew

Spicy Ostrich Stew

TSWANA (SWAH-NUH) 101

Tswana is a Bantu language and the national language of Botswana.

Some common Tswana words are:

1. Mane- Four

2. Eo- That

3. Leng- When

4. Na- Have

5. Tswa- From

6. Rata- Enjoy

7. Ura- Hour

8. Kwa- Other Side

9. Morwa- Son

10. Beke- Week

South African Bobotie (Meatloaf)

South Africa

Yield 3-5 servings

Ingredients:

1 cup whole milk

1 cup plain bread crumbs

2 pounds ground chuck

2 medium onions chopped

1 tablespoon sugar

½ cup raisins

6 dried apricots chopped

¼ cup lemon juice

1 teaspoon curry powder

1 tablespoon mango chutney

1 teaspoon salt

½ teaspoon black pepper

1 teaspoon turmeric

¼ cup beef stock

2 large eggs

Directions:

1. in a large mixing bowl, combine all the ingredients except one egg and ½ cup of milk. shape into meatloaf form

2. place bobotie in the slow cooker making a slight indentation in the middle

3. simmer on high 2 ½ -3 hours or low 5-6 hours or until a 160° F internal temperature is reached

4. using a bulb remove the fat beat the remaining egg with ½ cup milk and pour over the mixture and continue cooking on high another 30 minutes and on low 1 hour

5. top each serving with a spoonful of mango chutney if desired

Did you know: *South Africa has 9 provinces; Western Cape, Eastern Cape, Free State, Gauteng, KwaZulu-Natal, Limpopo, Mpumalanga, Northern Cape, North-West*

Seswaa

Botswana

Yield 6-8 servings

Ingredients:

2 pound chuck roast

2 teaspoons salt

1 ½ cups water

Directions:

1. in a slow cooker, add all the ingredients
2. simmer on high 4-5 hours or low 8-10 hours or until the roast reaches an internal temperature of 145° F
3. then pounded which resembles chopped or pulled meat

Note: In Botswana Seswaa is only seasoned with salt and cooked by the men of the village.

Did you know: *Botswana is a landlocked county with its population concentrated in eastern portion*

Kyinkyinga

Ghana

Yield 4-6 servings

Ingredients:

2 tablespoons olive oil

5 cloves garlic crushed

2 cups peeled yam cut into 1 " cubes

1 ½ pounds beef liver, cut into cubes

1chopped medium onion

3 chopped green bell peppers

1 cup raw peanuts

2 teaspoons fresh grated ginger

2 teaspoons paprika

2 cups vegetable stock

One 14 ounce can stew tomatoes

Directions:

1. in a slow cooker, add all the ingredients except tomatoes
2. simmer on high 3-4 hours or on low 6-8 hours
3. add tomatoes the last hour if cooking on low or 30 minutes if cooking on high

Did you know: *Ghana celebrates Independence Day from the United Kingdom on March 6th*

Lamb and Chickpea Tajine

North Africa

Yield 4-6 servings

Ingredients:

1 cup dried chickpeas

1 ½ pounds lamb

½ cup parsley

2 ribs of diced celery

1 cinnamon stick

1 teaspoon fresh grated ginger

2 teaspoons cayenne pepper

1 teaspoon turmeric

1 teaspoon coriander

2 cups lamb stock (or water)

One 14 ounce can stew tomatoes

Directions:

1. in a slow cooker, add all the ingredients except tomatoes
2. simmer on high 4-5 hours or on low 8-10 hours
3. add tomatoes the last hour if cooking on low or 30 minutes if cooking on high
4. remove cinnamon stick and serve

Did you know: *In Tunisia Arabic is the official language*

Rwandan Beef Stew

Rwanda

Yield 4-6 servings

Ingredients:

2 pounds stew beef cut into 1 " chunks

2 cups okra

1 medium onion chopped

2 large green plantains, peeled and cut into 1inch circles

1 teaspoon coriander

2 teaspoons salt

½ teaspoon black pepper

2 cups beef stock

10 whole ripe cherry tomatoes

Directions:

1. cut the tops of the okra and cut into bite size pieces
2. in a slow cooker, add all the ingredients
3. simmer on high for 4-5 hours or low for 8-10 hours
4. add tomatoes the last hour if cooking on low or 30 minutes if cooking on high

Did you know: *Rwanda is a tad smaller than the state of Maryland*

Beef Oxtail

West Africa

Yield 6-8 servings

Ingredients:

4 cloves of garlic crushed

3 pounds beef oxtail

2 medium onions sliced evenly

2 ribs of diced celery

1 cinnamon stick

1 teaspoon coriander

1 teaspoon salt

½ teaspoon black pepper

2 cups beef stock

Salt and pepper to taste

Directions:

1. in a slow cooker, add all the ingredients
2. simmer on high 5-6 hours or low 10-12 hours
3. remove cinnamon stick and serve

Did you know: *Liberia began as a settlement of freed slaves from the US in 1822*

Mushroom and Garlic Ostrich Stew

South Africa

Yield 6-8 servings

Ingredients:

3 cloves garlic crushed

2 pounds cleaned ostrich meat

1 medium onion, sliced

2 cups beef stock

Salt and pepper to taste

2 cups sliced crimini mushrooms

Directions:

1. in a slow cooker, add all the ingredients, except mushrooms
2. simmer on high for 3-4 hours or low for 6-8 hours, until ostrich is tender
3. add cleaned mushrooms the last hour if cooking on low or 30 minutes if cooking on high

Did you know: *In South Africa, the first multi-racial elections in 1994 ended apartheid*

Beef and Cassava Stew

East Africa

Yield 6-8 servings

Ingredients:

2 cups cassava (Yucca) cut into 1 " chunks

2 pounds stew beef cut into 1 " chunks

4 celery sticks, chopped

1 medium onion, sliced

½ teaspoon black pepper

2 cups beef stock

Salt and pepper to taste

2 cups sliced crimini mushrooms

15 whole ripe cherry tomatoes

Directions:

1. peel cassava and cut into even 1 inch chucks
2. add all ingredients except mushrooms and tomatoes to the slow cooker
3. simmer on high 4-5 hours or on low 8-10 hours
4. add tomatoes and mushrooms the last hour if cooking on low or 30 minutes if cooking on high

Did you know: *Uganda is a tad smaller than the state of Oregon*

Beef and Vegetable Stew

West Africa

Yield 6-8 servings

Ingredients:

½ cup dried chickpeas

3 cups butter nut squash cut into 1 " chunks

2 pounds stew beef cut into 1 " inch cubes

2 teaspoons Ethiopian Mit'mit'a spice mix

2 cups beef stock

2 medium ripe tomatoes, chopped

Directions:

1. peel squash, remove seeds and cut into even 1 inch chucks
2. add all ingredients except tomatoes to the slow cooker
3. simmer on high 4-5 hours or on low 8-10 hours
4. add tomatoes the last hour if cooking on low or 30 minutes if cooking on high

Did you know: *Togo is somewhat smaller than the state of West Virginia*

Spicy Ostrich Stew

South Africa

Yield 6-8 serving

Ingredients:

4 cloves garlic crushed

2 cups peeled yam cut into 1 " cubes

3 cups fresh kale

1 ½ pounds cleaned ostrich

1 teaspoon lemon juice

1 medium onion, sliced

2 teaspoons coriander

2 tablespoons red pepper flake

2/3 cup water

1 cup whole kernel corn

Salt and pepper to taste

Directions:

1. in a slow cooker, add all the ingredients
2. simmer on high 4-5 hours or low 8-10 hours
3. add corn the last hour if cooking on low or 30 minutes if cooking on high

Did you know: *The Rand is the currency of South Africa*

Lamb and Goat Stews

Botswana Goat Stew

Djibouti Stew

Lamb with Prunes

Kenyan Goat Stew

Peppered Lamb

Lamb Okra Stew

Bredie

Nigerian Goat Stew

Lamb Tajine with Dates and Almonds

Malawi Curry Goat

HAUSA (HOU-SAH) 101

Hausa is the national language of Niger; and also spoken in many other counties such as northern Nigeria, Benin, Burkina Faso, Cameroon, Chad, Congo, Eritrea, Ghana, Sudan and Togo.

Some common Hausa words are:

1. Àlkadàrii -Quality

2. Bàngaa -Drum

3. Alô -Hello

4. Àutaa -Child Youngest

5. Anàbii -Wine

6. Abinci Màì Daadii -Delicious Dish

7. Ìsa- Reach

8. Gsaa- Pride

9. Ìyaalìì -Family

10. Ùbaa -Father

Botswana Goat Stew

Botswana

Yield 6-8 servings

Ingredients:

1 cup baby carrots

1 small head of green cabbage

2 pounds of goat cut into 1 " cubes

1 cup chopped onions

Salt and pepper to taste

1½ cups goat stock

One 14 ounce can stew tomatoes

Directions:

1. add all ingredients in the slow cooker
2. simmer on high 4-5 hours or on low 8-10 hours
3. add tomatoes the last hour if cooking on low or 30 minutes if cooking on high

Did you know: *Botswana is somewhat smaller than the state of Texas*

Djibouti Stew

Republic of Djibouti

Yield 6-8 servings

Ingredients:

2 pounds of goat cut into 1 " cubes

1 cup chopped onions

1 cinnamon stick

1 teaspoon nutmeg

1 teaspoon cumin

1 teaspoon turmeric

¼ cup chopped parsley

1 ½ cups goat stock

Salt and pepper to taste

2 cups crimini mushrooms

Directions:

1. add all ingredients in the slow cooker
2. simmer on high 4-5 hours or on low 8-10 hours
3. add mushrooms the last hour if cooking on low or 30 minutes if cooking on high
4. remove cinnamon stick and serve

Did you know: *The nationality of the residents of Djibouti is Djiboutian*

Lamb with Prunes

Egypt

Yield 6-8 servings

Ingredients:

3 pounds lamb cut into 1 " cubes

1 cup baby carrots

1 cup chopped onions

1 ½ cups dried pitted prunes

2 teaspoons allspice

1 cinnamon stick

2 teaspoons cardamom

¼ cup chopped mint

2 cups lamb stock

Directions:

1. add all ingredients in the slow cooker
2. simmer on high 4-5 hours or on low 8-10 hours
3. add mushrooms the last hour if cooking on low or 30 minutes if cooking on high
4. remove cinnamon stick and serve
5.

Did you know: *The Library of Alexandria located in Alexandria, Egypt is the most famous library of the ancient world*

Kenyan Goat Stew

Kenya

Yield 4-5 servings

Ingredients:

5 cloves of garlic crushed

2 cups peeled yam cut into 1 " cubes

1 ½ pounds goat cut into 1 " cubes

1 cup chopped onions

2 heaping tablespoons tomato paste

1 tablespoon curry powder

2 cups goat stock

Salt and pepper to taste

One 14 ounce can stew tomatoes

Directions:

1. add all ingredients in the slow cooker
2. simmer on high 4-5 hours or on low 8-10 hours
3. add tomatoes the last hour if cooking on low or 30 minutes if cooking on high

Did you know: *Kenya is a bit more than twice the size of the state of Nevada*

Peppered Lamb

North Africa

Yield 3-4 servings

Ingredients:

5 cloves garlic crushed

2 pounds lamb cut into 1 " cubes

1 teaspoon mustard seeds

1 cinnamon stick

½ cup parsley

1 ½ teaspoons cumin

½ teaspoon black pepper

1 tablespoon coriander

2 cups lamb stock

1 cup pitted red olives

Directions:

1. add all ingredients in the slow cooker
2. simmer on high 4-5 hours or on low 8-10 hours

Did you know: *In Libya, more than 90% of the country is desert or semi desert*

Lamb Okra Stew

North Africa

Yield 4-6 servings

Ingredients:

4 cloves garlic crushed

2 cups fresh okra

2 pounds lamb cut into 1 " cubes

1 medium onion, chopped

2 teaspoons Harissa

2 cups lamb stock

½ teaspoon salt

2 medium fresh tomatoes evenly sliced

Directions:

1. cut the tops off the okra and cut into bite size pieces
2. in a slow cooker add ingredients except tomatoes cover and simmer on high for 4-5 hours or low for 8-10 hours
3. add tomatoes the last hour if cooking on low or 30 minutes if cooking on high

Did you know: *In Sudan, the lowest geographical point is the Red Sea*

Bredie

South Africa

Yield 5-6 servings

Ingredients:

3 cups fresh pumpkin cut into ½ " cubes

2 pounds lamb cut into 1 " cubes

1 medium onion, chopped

3 cups lamb stock

1 cinnamon stick

1 teaspoon nutmeg

1 bay leaf

Salt and pepper to taste

Directions:

1. add all ingredients in the slow cooker
2. simmer on high 4-5 hours or on low 8-10 hours
3. remove cinnamon stick and serve

Did you know: *South Africa surrounds the mostly black African county of Lesotho*

Nigerian Goat Stew

Nigeria

Yield 5-6 servings

Ingredients:

4 cloves of garlic crushed

3 pounds goat cut into 1 " cubes

1 cup baby carrots

1 cup chopped onions

1 bay leaf

1 teaspoon fresh grated ginger

1 tablespoon cayenne pepper

½ teaspoon black pepper

2 teaspoons piri piri (substitute cayenne pepper)

2 cups goat stock

Directions:

1. add all ingredients in the slow cooker
2. simmer on high 4-5 hours or on low 8-10 hours

Did you know: *Nigeria is a little more than twice the size of California*

Lamb Tajine with Dates and Almonds

North Africa

Yield 5-6 servings

Ingredients:

3 pounds lamb cut into 1 " cubes

1 medium onion, chopped

1 cinnamon stick

½ teaspoon black pepper

1 tablespoon coriander

¼ cup orange blossom honey

1 tablespoon lemon juice

1 cup unsalted almonds

2 cups lamb stock

1 ½ cups pitted dates

Directions:

1. add all ingredients except almonds into the slow cooker
2. simmer on high 4-5 hours or on low 8-10 hours
3. add almonds the last 30 minutes if cooking on high and the last hour if cooking on low
4. remove cinnamon stick and serve

Did you know: *Libya's capital is Tripoli*

Malawi Curry Goat

Malawi

Yield 4-5 servings

Ingredients:

3 pounds goat cut into 1 " cubes

4 cloves minced garlic

1 cup chopped onions

2 teaspoons Malawi Curry Powder

1 ½ cups goat stock

One 14 ounce can stew tomatoes

Directions:

1. add all ingredients in the slow cooker
2. simmer on high 4-5 hours or on low 8-10 hours
3. add tomatoes the last hour if cooking on low or 30 minutes if cooking on high

Did you know: *The official language of Malawi is English*

Not So Run of the Mill Stews

Pigeon Stew

Chicken Feet Stew

Mutton Apricot Stew

Stewed Sheep's Kidney

Sheep Head Stew

Elmussalammiya

LINGALA (LING-GAH-LA) 101

Lingala is the national language of the Democratic Republic of the Congo.

Some common Lingala words are:

1. Ti- Tea

2. Lilála- Orange

3. Mbula- Rain

4. Mesa- Table

5. Likei- Egg

6. Buku- Book

7. Míliki- Milk

8. Balabala- Street

9. Mbe- Flower

10. Loso- Rice

Pigeon Stew

Morocco

Yield 4-8 servings

Ingredients:

2 pounds cleaned pigeon

3 cloves garlic crushed

1 medium onion, slice

1 cinnamon stick

½ teaspoon saffron

2 cups vegetable stock

Salt and black pepper to taste

Directions:

1. in a slow cooker, add all the ingredients
2. simmer on high for 3-4 hours or low for 6-8 hours, until pigeon is tender
3. remove cinnamon stick and serve

Did you know: *Some of Morocco's major agricultural crops are citrus and olives*

Chicken Feet Stew

Ghana

Yield 3-4 servings

Ingredients:

1 pound chicken feet, cleaned

3 cloves garlic crushed

2 teaspoons piri piri (substitute cayenne pepper)

1 medium onion, sliced

2 cups chicken stock

Salt and black pepper to taste

One 14 ounce can stew tomatoes

Directions:

1. in a slow cooker, add all the ingredients
2. simmer on high for 4-5 hours or low for 8-10 hours, until greens are tender
3. add tomatoes the last hour if cooking on low or 30 minutes if cooking on high

Did you know: *The capital of Ghana is Accra*

Mutton Stew with Apricots

South Africa

Yield 4-8 servings

Ingredients:

1 ½ pounds mutton

1 cup dried apricots

3 cloves garlic crushed

1 medium onion, sliced

1 cup baby carrots

1 cinnamon stick

2 teaspoons ground ginger

2 teaspoons cardamom

2 cups vegetable stock

Salt and black pepper to taste

Directions:

1. in a slow cooker, add all the ingredients
2. simmer on high for 3-4 hours or low for 6-8 hours, until mutton is tender
3. remove cinnamon stick and serve

Did you know: *South Africa is a little less than twice the size of the state of Texas*

Stewed Sheep's Kidney

Morocco

Yield 6-8 servings

Ingredients:

2 cleaned Sheep's kidneys

1 medium onion, sliced

1 cinnamon stick

2 tablespoons coriander

½ cup chopped parsley

¼ cup lemon juice

½ teaspoon black pepper

2 cups vegetable stock

2 cups crimini mushrooms

Salt to taste

Directions:

1. cut each kidney lengthwise down the center evenly cutting each kidney in half
2. in a slow cooker add all the ingredients, except mushrooms cover and simmer on high for 3-4 hours or low for 6-8 hours, until kidneys are tender
3. add mushrooms the last hour if cooking on low or 30 minutes if cooking on high

Did you know: *Rabat is the capital of Morocco*

Sheep's Head Stew

Morocco

Yield 6-8 servings

Ingredients:

1 cleaned extra small sheep's head

3 medium peeled turnips

1 medium onion, sliced

½ cup chopped parsley

8 cups vegetable stock

1 cinnamon stick

2 tablespoons coriander

2 teaspoons ground ginger

Salt and black pepper to taste

Directions:

1. let the sheep's head soak in water for at least 2 hours
2. in a slow cooker add all the ingredients, cover and simmer on high for 4-5 hours or low for 8-10 hours, until sheep's tongue is tender
3. remove cinnamon stick and serve

Did you know: *Morocco's largest city is Casablanca*

Elmussalammiya

Sudan

Yield 2-4 servings

Ingredients:

6 cloves of garlic, crushed

1 pounds Sheep liver cut into ½ " slices

2 tablespoons red pepper

1 cup pitted dates

1 cup vegetable stock

Salt and pepper to taste

Directions:

1. in a slow cooker, add all the ingredients
2. simmer on high 1 ½- 2 hours on high or 3-4 hours on low until liver is tender

Did you know: *Sudan is the largest county in Africa*

Accompaniments

Fufu

Preserved Lemons

Coconut Rice

Pineapple Mango Chutney

Ugali

Date and Raisin Chutney

Spiced Rice

Pap

Pickled Limes

Mango Chutney

Tsamma Melon Preserves

Pickled Figs

CHEWA (CHEY-WAH) 101

Chewa is only one of the official languages of Malawi.

Some common Chewa words are:

1. Luma- To Bite

2. Bamba- Scale of Fish

3. Amba- To take its rise

4. Gwa- Firm

5. Dzoza- To anoint with oil

6. Enda- Flow

7. Bafa- Striking

8. Ipa- To be bad

9. Kali -Reaching up

10. Fuwa- Cooking stone

Fufu

West and Central Africa

Yield 3-4 servings

Ingredients:

2 large peeled yams cut into 1 " cubes (or one medium peeled cassava)

1 green plantain cut into ½ inch circles

2 cups water

½ teaspoon salt

Directions:

1. add all ingredients to the slow cooker
2. simmer on high 2-3 hours or low 4-6 or until yams and plantains are, fork tender
3. mash yams and plantains with a potato masher until smooth
4. allow mixture to cool slightly before handling. roll fufu into 1 inch balls, if mixture is not thick enough add a small amount of cornstarch

Note: Fufu usually served in a large communal bowls with soups or stews surrounding the fufu mound. With your thumb make an indentation in the middle of the fufu ball and use this as your utensil for eating

Did you know: *Liberia is slightly larger than the state of Tennessee*

(cf. Ja! p. 33)

Preserved Lemons

North Africa

Yield 1 quart jar

Ingredients:

4 medium lemons

½ cup salt

½ cup of water

Fresh squeezed lemon juice

Directions:

1. seal and sterilize jar according to the manufactures instructions
2. first slice lemons lengthwise in four equal sections without cutting though the entire lemon
3. open lemon slightly and pack the open sections inside with salt.
4. add lemons and water to the slow cooker, simmer on low 2-2½ hours
5. add each lemon to the jar using tongs and add enough lemon juice to cover to the top of the lemons leaving ¼ inch head room.
6. set aside to pickle for at least 3 weeks. every few days, turn jar over to mix lemon salt brine

Did you know: *Algeria's capital is Algiers*

Coconut Rice

North Africa

Yield 4-6 servings

Ingredients:

2 cups long grain, white rice

1 teaspoon sesame seeds

1 cup fresh grated coconut

1 teaspoon cumin seeds

2 cups water

1 teaspoon salt

1 tablespoon butter

Directions:

1. place all ingredients in a slow cooker
2. simmer on low for 5-6 hours

Did you know: *Tunisia's population is about 610,383,577*

Pineapple Mango Chutney

South Africa

Yield about 4 half pint jars

Ingredients:

1 large peeled ripe mango

One 20 ounce can crushed pineapple including ½ of the juice

1 medium onion, chopped

2 cloves garlic, crushed

1 teaspoon cinnamon

1 teaspoon nutmeg

1 tablespoon fresh grated ginger

1 teaspoon salt

1 tablespoon lemon juice

Directions:

1. seal and sterilize jars according to the manufactures instructions
2. combine ingredients in the slow cooker and simmer on high for 1 ½ - 2 hours or low 3-4 hours
3. pour into sterilized jars according to canning directions

Did you know: *South Africa's highest geographical point is Njesuthi Mountain 11,181 feet above sea level*

Ugali

East and West Africa

Yield 4-6 servings

Ingredients:

2 cups maize flour

3 ½ cups vegetable stock

½ teaspoon salt

Directions:

1. add all ingredients to the slow cooker
2. simmer on high 1 ½ -2
3. allow mixture to cool slightly before handling and roll into 1 inch balls

Note: Use the ugali like scoop to eat soups and to wrap around meats and vegetables stews

Did you know: *Comoros, Mauritius, and Seychelles are island African countries located in the Indian Ocean in the Eastern corridor of mainland Africa*

Date and Raisin Chutney

South Africa

Yield about 4 half pint jars

Ingredients:

3 cups pitted dates

1 cup golden raisins

1 medium onion, chopped

1 clove garlic, crushed

1 teaspoon paprika

1 tablespoon fresh grated ginger

1 teaspoon salt

½ cup white distilled vinegar

¼ cup water

Directions:

1. seal and sterilize jars according to the manufactures instructions
2. combine ingredients in the slow cooker
3. simmer on high for 2-2 ½ hours or low 4-5 hours
4. pour into sterilized jars

Did you know: *South Africa celebrates freedom day on April 27th*

Spiced Rice

North Africa

Yield 4-6 servings

Ingredients:

1 tablespoon butter

2 cups long grain, white rice

1 cinnamon stick

½ teaspoon ground cloves

1 teaspoon cumin seeds

2 cup water

1 teaspoon salt

Directions:

1. place all ingredients in a slow cooker
2. simmer on low for 5-6 hours
3. remove cinnamon stick and serve

Did you know: *Algeria is slightly less than 3½ times the size of Texas*

Pap

South Africa

Yield 5-6 servings

Ingredients:

2 cups white cornmeal

5 cups vegetable stock

1 drained can whole kernel corn

1 teaspoon salt

1 tablespoon butter

Directions:

1. add all ingredients to the slow cooker
2. simmer on high 2-3 hours or low 4-6

Did you know: *The Nationality of South Africa is South African*

Mango Chutney

(cf. Ja', p. 2a)

perhaps try p. 126: "Pineapple Mango Chutney"

South Africa

Yield about 3 half pint jars

Ingredients:

2 large ripe mangos peeled and sliced

½ cup raisins

1 cup medium diced onions

¼ cup minced fresh ginger

½ cup mango juice

2 tablespoons white distilled vinegar

1 ½ tablespoons curry powder

1 tablespoon red chili flakes

½ teaspoon cloves

½ cup granulated sugar

Directions:

1. seal and sterilize jars according to the manufactures instructions
2. place all ingredients into the slow cooker
3. simmer on high 2-3 hours or on low 4-6 hours
4. pour into sterilized jars

Did you know: *South Africa has 11 official languages*

Tsamma Melon Preserves

All of Africa

*Author's favorite recipe

Yields about 2 pint jars

Ingredients:

3 cups watermelon rind

2 cups of water

2 cups of sugar

½ cup lemon juice

1 teaspoon ginger

Directions:

1. sterilize and seal jars according to the manufacturer's instructions
2. remove green peel with a vegetable peeler or a knife leaving as little pink flesh as possible while removing all of the green skin
3. this should leave you with light green or white rind. cut rind into 1 inch cubes
4. add all ingredients into the slow cooker stir well and simmer 3 hours on high or 6 hours on low
5. rinds will appear slightly translucent
6. pour carefully and evenly into sterilized jars
7. rind will turn a natural lovely sunny yellow color

Did you know: *French is the official language of Senegal*

Pickled Figs

North Africa

Yields about 3 pint jars

Ingredients:

14 whole fresh figs cut in half (substitute dried figs)

2 cups of granulated sugar

2 tablespoons orange zest

1 ½ cups water

1 cup lemon juice

1 teaspoon picking salt

1 tablespoon distilled vinegar

1 sprig fresh mint leaves

Directions:

1. sterilize jar according to the manufacturer's instructions
2. wash and gently pat dry figs, remove stems and cut in half-lengthwise, place all ingredients in the slow cooker and gently stir
3. simmer on high 1-1 ½ hours or low 2-3 hours
4. without breaking figs carefully pour mixture evenly into mason jars leaving ¼ inch head room

Did you know: *Tunisia is the Northernmost County in Africa*

African Herbs and Spices 101

Herbs and Spices

Herbs and spices should be stored in airtight containers away from light and heat sources such as stoves and small appliances. Dried herbs and spices need to be replaced every six months since the older the herb or spice the less potent the flavor becomes. Keeping herbs and spices in the refrigerator does not increase their shelf life because the moisture from the refrigerator causes the dried herbs and spices to deteriorate faster. Some prepackaged herbs and spices list an expiration date however; do not be confused, this date is the "best when used by" date. Once the packaged herbs and spices have been, opened air is introduced into the product that causes the herbs and spices to weaken.

Herbs and spices should be replaced six months from the date of opening and not 6 months from the "best when used by" date. Some herb and spice companies have special websites to inform consumers of the herb and spice expiration date. Ground forms of herbs and spices loss their flavor quicker than those left whole. Whole dried herbs and spices can be used for up to a year as long as they are stored properly.

Common Herbs and Spices Used In African Cooking

African Bird Pepper- this pepper comes in a scorching 70,000 -150,000 Scoville Heat Units. African bird pepper, commonly referred to also as piri piri (pepper-pepper)

Allspice- a pea sized berry that is harvested unripe, dried, left whole, or ground into powder. The favor is robust and should be used in moderation.

Bay Leaf- strongly flavored and commonly a single bay leaf is used to flavor an entire soups or stews and remember to remove the bay leaf before serving.

Caraway- it is strongly flavored and should be used sparingly to enhance its flavor, lightly toast seeds before using.

Cardamom- has a gingery pine flavor and if using whole seeds crack before using.

Cinnamon- made of ground dried tree bark, sometimes left whole. Most of the cinnamon comes from trees of the "cinnamon cassia" family.

Cloves- easily cloves can overpower a dish due to a strong pungent, sweet intense flavor, especially when the cloves are in the ground, so use sparingly.

Coriander- the seed of the cilantro plant, the taste is citrus sweet flavor. The African counties of Morocco and Egypt produce a lot amount of the world's coriander.

Cumin- a member of the parsley family and has a strong earthy favor. During the middle ages, people believed that a joyful life would come to the bride and groom who carried Cumin seeds during the entire wedding ceremony.

Fennel Seed –mild licorice flavor also used to make tea; all parts of the plant are used in cooking and baking.

Fenugreek- extremely fragrant and the taste are robust, sweet, and a bit bitter. In cooking, there is not really a substitute for this unique spice.

Garlic- related to the lily family, grows in heads or clumps of cloves, and garlic is a relative of the onion. Cooks use garlic fresh and dried in recipes, garlic and has a strong favor and concentrated aroma.

Ginger- a clean, citrusy warm intense taste too much ginger translates to hot and spicy on the tongue. Ginger is one of the most popular spices in Africa.

Lemon Grass- has a strong citrus flavor, substitute for lemon zest in a recipe.

Mace- similar to nutmeg this is strong, spicy and warm to the taste, a little goes a long way.

Mint- adds a fresh taste to food; mint leaves are dried spearmint leaves and have a warm, fresh, sweet flavor.

Mustard seeds- have a pungent, bite and the seeds commonly used in preserves, soups, and stews. Africa has been using mustard for flavoring for thousands of centuries.

Nutmeg- sweet, nutty, heady fragrance and tastes warm and a bit sweet.

Paprika- a mild sweet red peppers in the Capsicum family and has a mild flavor and a vivid red color.

Parsley- one of the best-known herbs and adds a pleasant crisp fresh taste to African dishes.

Pepper Black & White- peppercorns are unripe berries of the piper nigrum vine. Black peppercorns are harvested just before ripeness and the berries are picked while still green, and dried. They have a hot, taste and abrasive aroma. For White Pepper, the berry is picked when fully ripe. The outer layer of skin is removed, leaving only the dried, kernel. White pepper has milder taste than that black pepper.

Saffron- the world's most expensive spice, Saffron threads are the stigma of the purple crocus and it takes 175,000-225,000 manually selected flowers to make a pound of saffron. Saffron has a strong aroma and a pungent, sweet taste and gives foods a brilliant yellow color.

Sesame seeds- a sweet, nutty flavor enhanced by toasting and the seeds are commonly harvested by hand.

Tamarind- native to the tropics of Africa tamarind is a brownish slightly sour tasting pod popular in Africa, Latin America, and the Caribbean.

Thyme-dried leaves of the mint family with earthy and minty overtones.

Turmeric- sharp, peppery, slightly musty, earthy aroma with an astringent flavor. Turmeric also adds a vivid yellow color to foods.

Index

Resources

About South Africa. (n.d.). Retrieved 8 23, 2007, from The Republic of South Africa: http://www.southafrican.za.net/about-sa.html

African Business Development Association. (n.d.). ABDAS. Retrieved 1 24, 2008, from African Business Development Association: http://www.abdas.org/geography.html

Agency, C. I. (2007, 8 24). reference of maps Africa. Retrieved 2 3, 2008, from cia.gov: https://www.cia.gov/library/publications/the-world-factbook/reference_maps/africa.html

Ager, S. (n.d.). Southern Sotho (Sesotho). Retrieved 2 28, 2008, from http://www.omniglot.com/writing/sesotho.htm

All Africa Global Media. (n.d.). All Africa. Retrieved 5 24, 2007, from All Africa: http://allafrica.com/

Bantu quotes, W. o. (n.d.). World of quotes. Retrieved 12 14, 2007, from www.worldofquotes.com/proverb/bantu/1/index.html- Bantu proverb

Bayley, M. (1971). Black Africa Cookbook. San Francisco: Determined Productions, Inc.

Botswana Embassy. (n.d.). Botswana Embassy Japan. Retrieved 3 4, 2008, from Botswana Embassy: http://www.botswanaembassy.or.jp/culture/body5.html

Embassy of Sudan South Africa. (n.d.). Embassy of Sudan South Africa. Retrieved 12 31, 2007, from Sudanese Food: http://www.sudani.co.za/people_tradition_food.htm

Gordon-Smith, C. (2000). Flavoring with Herbs. In C. Gordon-Smith, Flavoring with Herbs (pp. 6, 8, 9). London: Ryland Peters and Small.

Government of British Columbia. (n.d.). Farm Products A-Z. Retrieved 3 3, 2008, from Beans: http://www.agf.gov.bc.ca/aboutind/products/plant/beans.htm

http://www.websters-online-dictionary.org/. (n.d.). http://www.websters-online-dictionary.org/. Retrieved 4 28, 2008, from http://www.websters-online-dictionary.org/: http://www.websters-online-dictionary.org/

Library of Congress. (n.d.). Retrieved from Digital Collections & Services: http://memory.loc.gov/pp/pphome.html

McCormick. (n.d.). The Enspicelopedia. Retrieved 3 8, 2008, from McCormick Spice Encyclopedia: http://www.mccormick.com/content.cfm?ID=8291

News, T. B. (n.d.). Country profile: Ghana. Retrieved 12 14, 2007, from The BBC News: http://news.bbc.co.uk/1/hi/world/africa/country_profiles/1023355.stm

Osseo-Asare, F. (2005). Food Culture in Sub-Saharan Africa. West Port: Greenwood Press.

Rambuwani, L. D. (n.d.). Diospyros lycioides Desf. . Retrieved 9 12, 2007, from Plantz Africa: http://www.plantzafrica.com/plantcd/diospyroslyc.htm

Sheasby, A. (2003). The Book of Slow Cooking. New York: Berkley Publishing Group.

State of Victoria. (n.d.). Food culture and religion. Retrieved 10 10, 2007, from http://www.betterhealth.vic.gov.au/bhcv2/bhcarticles.nsf/pages/food_culture_and_re ligion?opendocument

The BBC News. (n.d.). Country profile: Algeria. Retrieved 11 30, 2007, from The BCC News: http://news.bbc.co.uk/2/hi/middle_east/country_profiles/790556.stm

The BBC News. (n.d.). Country profile: Democratic Republic of Congo. Retrieved 12 12, 20077, from http://news.bbc.co.uk/2/hi/africa/country_profiles/1076399.stm

The BBC News. (n.d.). Country profile: Lesotho. Retrieved 11 24, 2007, from http://news.bbc.co.uk/2/hi/africa/country_profiles/1063291.stm

The Good Food BBC. (n.d.). The Good Food. Retrieved 2 17, 2008, from The Good Food: http://www.bbcgoodfood.com//

The Great American Spice Company. (n.d.). Herbs and Spices. Retrieved 3 7, 2008, from The Great American Spice Company: http://www.americanspice.com/catalog/spices/0Z.html?_ssess_=b8fd7a9568093dbe8 bcf89c52a6270e9

US Department of State. (n.d.). Eritrea. Retrieved 3 11, 2008, from US Department of State Bureau of African Affairs: http://www.state.gov/r/pa/ei/bgn/2854.htm

World-Newspapers. (n.d.). World newspapers. Retrieved 11 15, 2007, from Africa: http://www.world-newspapers.com/africa.html

Zamouri spices. (n.d.). Moroccan Flavors. Retrieved 3 10, 2008, from Zamouri spices: http://www.zamourispices.com/section1.html?gclid=CKTluY3k_pECFR6CkwodNX9 P3Q

Photo Credits

Photos on front and back cover taken and copyright by the author

Unnumbered introduction page of schoolchildren courtesy of USAID photographer Chris Thomas www.USAID.gov

Unnumbered introduction page of women walking with basket on her head photographer PACT www.USAID.com

Unnumbered introduction page of men in boat courtesy of USAID photographer K. Burns www.USAID.gov

Unnumbered introduction page of schoolchildren courtesy of USAID photographer Chris Thomas www.USAID.gov

Unnumbered introduction page of family working courtesy of USAID photographer A. Fleuret www.USAID.gov

Page X Courtesy of USAID photographer unknown, www.USAID.gov

Page XII Courtesy of USAID photographer A. Fleuret, www.USAID.gov

Page IX Courtesy of USAID photographer unknown, www.USAID.gov

Page XI Courtesy of USAID photographer S. Poland, www.USAID.gov

Page 14 Courtesy of USAID photographer unknown, www.USAID.gov

Page 15 Courtesy of USAID photographer S. Kalscheur www.USAID.gov

Page 133 Courtesy of USAID photographer Laura Lartigue www.USAID.gov

Page 134 Courtesy of USAID photographer Richard Nyberg www.USAID.gov

Page 135 Courtesy of USAID photographer unknown, www.USAID.gov

Page 136 Courtesy of USAID photographer Ken Wiegand, www.USAID.gov

Page 146 Courtesy of USAID photographer unknown, www.USAID.gov

Page 147 Courtesy of USAID photographer unknown, www.USAID.gov

Page 148 Courtesy of USAID photographer unknown, www.USAID.gov

Page 150 Courtesy of USAID photographer unknown, www.USAID.gov

Page 151 Courtesy of USAID photographer unknown, www.USAID.gov

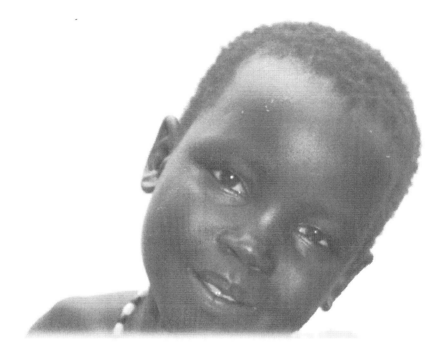

"Even silence speaks"

-Nigerian Proverb

"Only the mountains never meet"

-Namibian Proverb

"The eyes of a wise person see all"

-Tanzanian Proverb

"What you see in yourself is what you see in the world"
-African Proverb

"Trees that are together brush
against each other"
-Togolese Proverb

"Inside a small seed hides a large tree"
-African Proverb

A Note about the Author

Ivy Newton-Gamble is a graduate of Florida A & M University earning a B.A. in Sociology. She is also an avid reader and traveler fascinated by people and African cultural traditions. She currently lives in Florida tending to her garden of organically grown fruits and vegetables and is a proud member of

Zeta Phi Beta Sorority Inc.

5589464R0

Made in the USA
Lexington, KY
25 May 2010